GUTTED

A play by Sharon Byrne

PRETTY PUG PUBLISHING

EST. 2020

ISBN 978-1-8382149-4-4
First published in 2021 by Pretty Pug Publishing

Pretty Pug Publishing
26 The Seed Warehouse
Poole Quay BH15 1SB

© Sharon Byrne 2021

All rights reserved. Except for the purpose of review, no part of this book may be reproduced, stored in a retireval system or transmitted in any form or by any means, electronic, mechanical, photocopying, recording or otherwise, without the prior consent of the publisher.

WITH SPECIAL THANKS TO:

All the cast and crew of Gutted.

Nicola Samer	Director	2017
Chris White	Director	2018 / 2019
Sarah Horner	PR & Marketing	2017
Pippa Ailion	Casting	2017
Marianne McConnell	Designer	2017 / 2018
Jennifer Rooney	Movement	2017
Jo Kornstein	Set Designer	2017
Zoe Burnham	Lighting Designer	2017
Phil Wilson	Sound Designer	2017
Max Heller	Stage Managment	2017
Sorcha Corcoran	Costume Designer	2017 / 2018 / 2019

Cast 2017
Lucia McAnespie
Rose O'Laughtlin
Nancy Sullivan

Cast 2018/19
Niamh Finlay
Eleanor Byrne
Sarah Hosford
Sophie Sood — Production Manager
Vivienne Foster — Producer
Natalie Gallagher — Casting
(for Pippa Ailion)
Marty Langthorne — Lighting Design
Jess Tucker Boyd — Movement Director

Lesley Vickerage — An amazing human being
Fran McGuire — PR
Emma Martin — Marketing
Marianne McConnell — Graphic Design
Michaela Corcoran — Stage Manager

Paula Gillespie & The Marlowe Theatre and their amazing team

The Umbrella Cafe   **Mettyears Salon**
George Lister, Samphire   **Tell Tails**
First Degree East

And *a very special thanks* to my family anf local community of Whitstable who helped to fund Gutted, and get this project off the ground and who came to see Gutted at the Marlowe Theatre, Canterbury. Amazing individuals.

Many Thanks,
Sharon

GLOSSARY

To those of you unfamilar with the Irish language and Irish Slang terms *[Publisher Edit: I was one of them!]* we have put together a small glossary of terms to help you out:

Gee, Fanny	Vagina
A ride	A fuck
Spare	Crazy
Harp	Brand of Irish beer
Tayto	Brand of Irish crisps
Eejit	Thick or stupid person
Tuppence	Two pence
Scarlet	Embarrassed
Not the full shilling	Mentally unstable
Craic	Fun
Hidings	Beatings / To beat someone up
Reefs	Pulls up or out
Corporation	Council
Sap	Idiot
Wearing	Kissing or snogging
Gardai	The Irish Police
Confession	Confessing to a priest
Debs	Short for Debunates Ball (Prom)
Bowzy	A low-class mean or obstreperous person
Gypo	A gypsy / A traveller
Mountjoy / Joy	A prison in Dublin

GUTTED
In Production

Gutted was first performed at the Marlowe theatre on the 24th September 2017 and directed by Nicola Samer.

Breda was played by Lucia McAnespie. Deirdre by Rose O'Laughlin and Delores by Nancy Sullivan.

Gutted went on to perform in Edinburgh at the Edinburgh Fringe Festival in 2018.

It was directed by Chris White. Breda was played by Eleanor Byrne, Deirdre by Niamh Finlay and Delores by Sarah Hosford.

Gutted also toured in the South East and London also directed by Chris White and played by Eleanor Byrne, Niamh Finlay and Sarah Hosford to critical acclaim.

Gutted was supported by the Marlowe theatre, The Arts Council England, Canterbury City Council.

Gutted

For my mum, Anne Yaverbaum

and my son, Leyton Solomon Byrne

♥

Gutted
by Sharon Byrne

Gutted

Character List

Delores O'Bryan	Teens
Deirdre O'Hanlon	Teens
Breda Delaney	Early twenties

All minor characters are played by the above 3 main characters throughout the play.

Asumpta	Teens
Malachy McEvoy	Forties
Jerry Kavanagh	Early Teens
Luke O'Hanlon	Brother
Elvis	Late forties
Rowena	Early twenties
Imelda Finnegan	Teens
Noreen O'Dyer	Teens

The play is set in a Fish Factory and works as a series of three intwerwoven monolgues from Delores, Breda, Deirdre.

Lighting is used to highlight the characters and changes of scene.

All stage directions *shown in italics* are suggestions only.

SCENE 1.

A fish factory in 1980's Dublin. Enter Delores, Deirdre and Breda. The women prepare for work. They put on their work coats, blue hair nets, aprons and wellingtons. When they are ready they stand stage front, facing the audience with a look of disdain.

They begin to gut fish. Tainted Love comes on the radio and the girls sing along to it.

DELORES. So I said to her. You ask him, I'm not. NO, she said. I'm not fucking asking him. You ask him. So I said. NO. YOU fucking ask him. And it went on and on and on. I was knackered from it. She gave in, in the end, she did. Asumpta asked Malachy, our boss, for half a day off so we could go to the debs. And what do ye think he fucking said? The fucker said no, the cheek of him. NO? Well I was going mad.

MOTHER. I'm going out soon you two and I don't want any smoking in this house, do ye hear me?

DEIRDRE. It was a Saturday night. Me and Luke always looked forward to Saturday nights, cause that's when the babysitter Rowena came around. Rowena was brill, dead easy going. She'd let me stay up real late and do whatever we wanted. She even let me smoke. Just me, not Luke. No, no, definitely not Luke. There'd be big trouble if me Ma ever found out.

BREDA. He was Italian, had a Ferrari and a chip shop in Howth. I couldn't believe it, couldn't believe me luck. I'd only split up with Rocky a couple of months ago. That fucking bowzy of a husband. I was going to AA and working here at the time.

Gutted

SCENE 2.

DELORES. It was a big night out. Everyone was going. We were even going and it wasn't even our debs for Christ sake. And he said nope, we couldn't have a fuckin' day off. What did we think this place was, Butlin's or something? I'd never even been to Butlin's, let alone anywhere else. The furthest I'd ever been was Funderland, the only theme park we had, over in Balls Bridge after Christmas. He wouldn't even give us a lousy fuckin' half-day off. I'd had two years of this place, never even been sick. Two years of cleaning out guts and blood of stinking fish and every kind of fish as well. Sure I know what every fish looks like inside and out. The one's that smirk at ya. The miserable ones. Jaysus *(laughs)* those one's make ye feel rotten- like you've just murdered your own sister or something. I mean two fucking years of putting dinner on people's fuckin' tables all over Dublin. And what thanks do I get? We took it in the end. Yeah we did. And no we didn't feel guilty. We got one of the girls to clock out for us.

Looking behind her to the other girls.

Ye see, we knew the boss was having it off with Imelda Finnegan from packaging and sure we thought if he found out, we could always blackmail 'im. Threaten to tell his wife like. *(Laughs)* That day we left work, and walked across the North road. The North Road goes all the way up to the North of Ireland. When I was a kid, I use to think that it was just up the road, only five minutes like. *(Laughs)* And it scared me, yeah it did, coz I thought all those shootings and bombings were only next door. On a Sunday, I'd go to mass just to get the fuck away, and I'll tell you, I was terrified, coz I thought I'd get shot just for going to mass. Every day on the news there was somebody getting killed.

Beat.

We crossed over the road and went through the gap, where all the graffiti was. 'Up the IRA' and 'Fuck the British' was permanently written on those walls. The young fella's were always writing that sort of stuff on the walls. They didn't even know what they were writing. They were just listening to other silly shites who didn't even know what they were saying. All they knew was that it was bad to like the English and that if you didn't hate them you got your head kicked in. Fucking eejits. We didn't care about what was going on up North. We were too busy getting on with our own lives. So, we walked through the gap and who was there? Only Jerry Kavanagh.

Beat.

Jerry Kavanagh's a real WANKER. Everyone hates him. He's got red hair and he's as ugly as sin. None of the girls around our way fancy him and the gas thing about that is that, well he really fancies himself. And who can fuckin' blame him really? *(Laughs and laughs)* I mean what else do you do when no one fancies you? He didn't give a shite about what people thought. I mean, it's a bit odd to be so arrogant when you're so ugly like.

JERRY. Give us a look at your fanny ye gypo. Go on, I dare ye.

DELORES. The dirty bastard and the state of him. I couldn't believe it; me with me blue coat on, me cap and me wellies. Jesus a sight for sore eyes. But there you go, that's desperation for you.

ASUMPTA. *(towards off stage)* Get lost. You dirty bastard. And what does he do? WELL he only takes his prick out and starts pulling himself off in front of us. Jaysus Christ. We were mortified but we couldn't stop laughing when we saw the size of it. *(Laughs)* JAYSUS The last time I saw a prick like that was when one of me brothers was two.

JERRY. *(off stage)* Go on, yiz -slags. Your fanny stinks of trout.

DELORES. And then he laughs his head off like a madman.

Delores turns to face Deirdre stage left.

SCENE 3.

Deirdre stands centre stage with her hands in her pockets.

DEIRDRE. Rowena was a bit stricter with him. But sometimes, yeah sometimes Rowena gave him a drag of her fag. Luke thought he was rapid when she did that. Made him feel real big. Sure he thought he was James Bond when he did it, until he coughed his guts up. All he needed was a dry martini and he was away.. And sure he was a little dwarf for his age so a drag couldn't do him any harm if ya know what I mean. And anyway he wanted to be a jockey, what was the big deal? Rowena came round around 8. Me Ma didn't really trust me on my own with Luke.

MOTHER. No Deirdre. You're too young to babysit Luke.

DEIRDRE. I was 15 going on 30 for Christ sake. I was already working in this dive of a place.. I think she was afraid I'd bring a fella round and get pregnant like half the other girls on our road. Sure I hadn't even done it yet. Well not all the way anyway. I wanted to go on the pill right cos I met this fella and jaysus was he bloody gorgeous or what and I wanted to ride him but he was married.

SALLY. Shouldn't let that stop ya...

DEIRDRE. Me friend said, Terrible! I know. So I told me Ma I was still a virgin but she wouldn't believe me cos she found the pill in me bag! I know fucking mortified or what?! I told her I was minding it for me friend Sally at school cos she didn't want her Ma to know she was on the pill. Now of course it was me taking it, but I couldn't tell her, she'd go spare! Ma asked me where she got it and I told her I said she got it from her doctor, a woman doctor who was very open minded.

Gutted

MOTHER. Open minded is right, up her own fucking arse, more
   like.

DEIRDRE. For god's sake she went turning it into a right big
   drama. Wasn't falling for it. So I had to make more shite
   up, I told her Sally was having problems with her periods
   and that's why she was taking it. The doctor wouldn't
   give it to her otherwise. Ma knew you could only get it on
   prescription, and most doctors didn't believe in giving it to
   us young girls, girls like me self, any fucking girls if ye ask
   me. But anyways getting back to that night. Luke, like the
   Roger Moore he is, runs and opens the door for Rowena.
   Nothing to do with fancying the pants of her. For gods sake,
   she was twice his age. He was always sayin' -

LUKE. When I'm ten I'm going to ask Rowena to marry me.

DEIRDRE. And Every time she came round to babysit he'd try
   to make her watch the Six Million Dollar Man, as if that was
   going to impress her like. I tried to tell her that girls aren't
   really into that but he didn't understand. I couldn't tell him
   that all we wanted was to get off with a fella cos it's out
   of this world. He was too young. Anyway, Rowena watched
   it to keep him happy but you could tell she was bored out
   of her brains chain smoking one Major after another.
   I tried to tell her not to do it cos she'd end up with cancer
   like Mrs O'Hara down the road but she wouldn't listen.
   Anyway we watched a bit of television, then made the jelly
   for the trifle. We always had trifle after dinner on a Sunday
   and I loved making it. I loved the jelly. I loved watching it
   change and get all wobbly like. I loved the strawberry
   flavour, and how it melted down into the hot water, and I
   loved drinking it too, it tasted a bit like Ribena and to be
   honest, it was just something to do. But Rowena looked
   different that night. It was peculiar. Her hair was all blonde
   and silky like the girl in the Sun Silk advert. Except, hers
   was a bit more gingery looking. She wore a red corduroy

skirt and a green jumper and had a cut on her knee. I always expected her to have a cut or a bruise or something from all the roller skating she did. Rowena went disco roller skating every week and she always said she'd take me but she never did. I lived in hope.

MOTHER. I'll be down in a minute. I'm nearly ready.

DEIRDRE. Me Ma had a date with some fella she met down the local. Ma and Da had just split up for the fiftieth time or whatever. I was now so used to it that when it was announced, I just shrugged. When I'd run into me Da he was always saying he'd come round but he never did and when he did, me Ma just roared at him.

MOTHER. Get out of here ye fucking bastard. I hate your guts.

DEIRDRE. Then me and Luke would join in with her.

ALL. Get out of here ye fucking bastard.

DEIRDRE. He pushed me Ma down the stairs that time. That's the last time I saw him until... after what happened that night *(Pause)* Anyway, Rowena kept on chain smoking, she was in her own world. Then Rowena started crying. We couldn't believe it. Rowena was always happy, there was never a dull moment but that night she said she wished she was Wonder Woman so she could twirl around like her and turn into someone new. Later on me Ma came down and saw how upset Rowena was, so took her out of the room and into the hall way.

Deirdre pretends to listen through a gap in the door.

ROWENA. I think I'm pregnant Mrs O'Dwyer and I don't know what I'm going to do.

MOTHER. Try not upset yourself Rowena. Listen to me, things can be done these days. We'll talk later okay. So calm yourself down. It'll be alright. Look if anyone comes round, don't open the door and for Christ sake don't let their Da in. And by the way, no cigarette smoking in the sitting room.

ROWENA. I can't tell me mother, please don't say anything, she'll kill me.

MOTHER. Rowena, I won't tell a soul. If it makes you feel better, there's loads of Tayto in the press, so help yourself to them. And there's a can a' Harp in the fridge. That'll cheer you up.

DEIRDRE. Just at that moment, there was a knock at the door. The door opens, then we saw him... me Ma's fella. Well Jaysus Mother of God he was disgusting looking. He looked like a horrible ugly version of Elvis, only uglier. He had a massive mole right smack bang in the middle of his nose. We stood there in shock. Me Ma slapped us back into the living room and told us to stop staring. But we couldn't help it... Me Ma put on her fake fur and off they went. We were mortified, Rowena stopped crying, from the sheer shock of it all. Then the doorbell rang again.

SCENE 4.

Breda looks down at herself and points to what she is wearing. A loud siren rings out.

SUPERVISOR *(off stage and shouting)*. Get back to work!

BREDA. I didn't really want to get involved with anyone
 again, but I couldn't help myself. I was fed up. I needed
 a bit of attention and a bit of you know what, and sure
 jaysus to be honest with you now, I was dying for it. I met
 the Italian stallion the night I went out with the girls,
 well, not the girls, more like owl' ones really. We all went
 out. Me, me Sister-in-law Clare, I know, you get on even
 when you're not all that keen on each other, and me
 friend Noreen. Noreen's one of me best friends. She's
 married as well. She's got three kids. Three boys, Darren,
 John and Finbarr, all gorgeous looking. They play with
 my two Ciara and Anthony. Only live round the block.
 Jesus I've known Noreen since I was crawling around
 in nappies. We grew up on the same road and went
 to St. John's together. Sure we had great fun tormenting
 the nuns at our school. Oh we hated them. *(Laughs)* They
 used to force us to drink half pints of milk for fuck sake.
 Half pints of milk that were thick with sour cream on
 the top. And those corn beef sandwiches too. Jaysus they
 were horrible, worse than the milk. They had a layer of
 thick grease across the inside of them, and they were
 always freezing cold. They'd freeze the gums off you. You
 wouldn't even give them to a dead dog, let alone a kid. And
 if that wasn't bad enough at break time in the winter we
 used to be shiverin' out in the yard, just dying to get back
 into the school, and they wouldn't let us in until that
 fuckin' bell went. Not even if you were dying for the toilet.
 Those bitches. I'll tell you one thing for absolutely nothing,
 we've never forgotten St Johns. I could go on and go on but

Gutted

I won't bore ya with all that Catholic codswallop. Anyway, Noreen came from a small family, unusual, and I came from a big one, not unusual.

Beat.

Noreen? Oh me Ma was very fond of Noreen. In all honesty now, I think she was fonder of her, than she was of me. *(Laughs)* As if me Ma didn't have enough kids to worry about. They were walking out on their own. There was the five boys, Jerro, Stevo, Seano, Jimmy and Shay. And the six girls, Me, Teresa, Cathleen, Imelda, Tara, and Joan. Fucks sake, that's enough. I don't know how me Ma gave birth to all of us. Maybe she didn't, who knows? *(Laughs)* Me brothers are mad like me Da. Alco's, always in the pub, always getting into fights. Swine's, they are. Me Da's always called them, the little swine's.

DA. Ah come here you little swine's ya. Come over here and give us a kiss.

BREDA. With a big sloppy mouth on him and all. Sure the poor little things couldn't even walk. A lazy bollox he was, fuck sake. He'd sit there watching the Saturday races; Grandstand or whatever you call it... Shouting through the hole in the wall to me Ma.

DA. Make us a cup-a-tea Rosaline, I'm fucking parching I am.

BREDA. Lazy bollox. Me brothers are the same. My Ma did everything for them, so they can't do anything for themselves. Eejits. And cause of them, people from our road think I'm the same. Sure there was a time when I couldn't walk past any of the girls on our road before they'd let it down the road afraid for their life. Stupid! I pretended I didn't care, but I did. I really did. I don't really like coming from a rough family, but you can't choose who your family are going to be now. Can you?

SCENE 5.

Delores picks up a bright pink debutantes dress, hangs it around her neck swishes around in it.

DELORES. We got away from Jerry Kavanagh. And when we got home to Asumpta's, her Ma was doing dinner. A bit of bacon, cabbage and potato. Her Ma always doing bacon, cabbage and potato, Asumpta's sick of it. It's either that or sausages and rashers or liver. Asumpta says that she's going to turn into a sausage one day; a bit like Jerry Kavanaghs, if she has to eat anymore. *(Laughs)* Her Ma never cooks the fish we brings home, unless its cod and she's even very particular about that. That has to be boiled in a pot with some onions.

ASUMPTA. It's absolutely fucking delicious.

DELORES. Of course, we managed to get out of the dinner and went upstairs to get ready. And there hanging on the front of Asumpta's wardrobe, was our dresses; a cream one and a shocking pink one, full of frills. We put them on and whished around the room in them.

Delores and Asumpta turn around in the dresses.

We were dead excited to think, that in a couple of hours, we'd be dressed up to the nines like Cinderella going to the ball.

Tainted Love chorus plays. They sing and dance to it.

DECO *(off stage and banging on door)*. Turn that fucking down. Turn it down or I'll come in there and smash it up.

Gutted

DELORES. We stopped but you wouldn't believe it- the nutter went into his room and started belting out, A Bat out of Hell. Jumping around his room like a fucking maniac. We didn't dare tell him to shut up, because he'd break your bleedin' neck. You didn't mess with Deco. He was a nut case.

DEIRDRE. It's nearly seven and the fella's turn up to the house, to pick us up. We leg it downstairs cause we have to go to the Green, where everyone is being picked up by the bus. The bus that's taking us to St Augusta's, where the debs is being held. A very posh do, very posh. And then typical, just as we're about to go, Asumpta realizes she's left her shoes at the factory. There's a big drama about this. But then her Ma goes up the stairs, we follow, like follow the fecking leader. She goes into her room, and believe it or not but she takes out her old wedding shoes and gives them to Asumpta. It makes me want to cry cause, my Ma wouldn't give me anything, wouldn't give me tuppence. My Ma's a mean bitch, forty five and I was one too many for her. The shoes, oh the shoes are immaculate and they fit and they finish her fuchsia pink off beautifully. Asumpta dries her eyes and the panic is over and then the doorbell rings. We leg it down the stairs again, knackered and sweating now, and Asumpta's Da is already opening the door to the two fella's we're going with. And then there's a big silence... It was Anto Keogh and Tomo Burke and they were all dressed up to the nines, in black suits and dickey bows, and Jesus we were mortified and they were mortified. We were all scarlet! By the way I'm with Anto, the better looking one, and Asumpta's with Tomo. And well, Tomo, let's put it this way, he's not the full shilling, but Asumpta was happy.

SCENE 6.

Deirdre still in blue coat, cap and wellingtons, holds an 80's walkman in her hand with earphones round her neck. An 80's track plays in the background.

DEIRDRE. Rowena's boyfriend Paddy barges in with a few of his friends. I'll never forget it, it was rapped. We stayed up, had the craic with them.. I knew I shouldn't have been there, if me ma knew she'd have killed me. Killed us all. But I was having a great time. I had a bit of a laugh with Paddy's friend Brian and he was bloody gorgeous. We were listening to some of me Ma and Da's old records. Tom Jones and that, having a bit of a dance on the living room floor. It was brilliant. But it wasn't long until that came to an end when Rowena saw Brian trying to get off with me. He was doing nothing. But she gave me a slap round the head and told me to fuck off up to bed. I was sooooo pissed off. I could hear everyone laughing, having a great time. They were fucking getting louder and louder as well. And I could smell the cigarette smoke coming up the stairs. Me Ma told Rowena she couldn't smoke in the house let alone have fellas round. I was terrified she'd come back any minute and there'd be big trouble. But she didn't. I kind of wish she had now.

Gutted

SCENE 7.

BREDA. At the time everyone thought I was mad, mad for leaving Rocky. Rocky was my brother Seano's best friend. He fancied me for years. And then one night we got off with each other. A few weeks later, I found out I was up the duff. That was it. Me life was mapped out for me. I had Ciara first. She's six now and then Anthony. He's five, only a year between them. Then got preggers again - lost that one thank God. God forgive me for sayin' that. But if you saw what he put me through, then you wouldn't blame me for saying it.

Breda turns to face Noreen.

He's never going to change Noreen

NOREEN. I know, he's a waster Breda. You have got to get away from him. One of these days he'll kill you.

Breda turns back to the audience

BREDA. She knew about the hidings and the drugs. She didn't blame me. I had to get away from Rocky and I'd do ANYTHING.

They sing together.

SCENE 8.

Deirdre opens her coat, and rubs her stomach. Deirdre alone. A light beams huge behind her. Her shadow seems small.

DEIRDRE. You see it's still a bit blurry like and I still can't figure out what really happened after that. But I remember falling asleep, I was knackered from that can of Harp I had. Luke was definitely asleep coz he was in the other bed over the other side of the room. At some point, later on, I woke up again and I heard a lot of shouting and it was Rowena arguing with her fella.

PADDY. No fuckin' way, ye can't be. It's not fucking mine. Could be anyone's. You're a slag.

DIERDRE. The door slammed and he was gone and she kept crying, but I didn't go down coz she would just tell me to go back up again. I eventually fell asleep. It must have been a deep sleep because then ages after. I don't know what time it was, coz I... I, like I said, it was all a bit blurry and dark, but I felt a sudden heaviness on me bed, like an extra duvet but only heavier and I tried... I tried to turn, but it was too dark and I couldn't see what it was or who? And then I tried to say something, but then this big hand came over nearly my whole face. And I couldn't make a sound, and I suddenly nearly shit meself. I was paralysed, afraid to move... couldn't move... and then I heard this voice whispering in my ear whispering in my ear: Shushhhhhhh, shush don't make a sound. Shush, shushshshshsh, now you don't want to wake up your little brother. So I didn't move. I froze and imagined all sorts of things and I tried... I tried, really fucking tried to scream, but I couldn't... just couldn't. I thought I was dreaming, couldn't believe it.....couldn't believe what was happening, And then I could feel him pulling down the covers and then I was freezing, and It dawned on me.

Gutted

Beat.

The space darkens and a shadow appears in the light behind her.. And we see a hand slowly reach over as if to cover her face.

I tried to free me arms but he was too heavy and in the dark I could feel. See his shadow over my bed and I knew what was coming next but. But it's... *Beat.*

His shadow darkens over me and then... well... he's... And I try to stop him, but I can't cause he's too strong and then he reefs up my nightdress and before I know what hits me, he's... and still covering my mouth with his hand, so I won't scream and it's quick and after a few thrusts it's over. *(Angrily)* He then quickly pulls away and covers me up again in the dark and leaves the room very quickly, and then I can suddenly breathe again, but I'm hot, very, very, hot and I feel very strange, and I try to... want to scream but I can't. Because I think that I'm dreaming, and that this hasn't happened, THIS HASN'"T HAPPENED TO ME. And then I turn around to check to see if Luke is still asleep, afraid that he might've heard or saw something. I wanted to go out of the room. I did. I wanted to scream. But I couldn't, it was too late. He was gone.

Beat. She roars. Mam! Mam!

MOTHER: What love, What love....What's the matter?

DEIRDRE. I tried to tell 'er. I did. I really did but she was still drunk and she just kept saying it was all a bad dream, and just kind of shushed me to sleep again. I tried again. I told her there was someone in the room but she just kept saying it was a bad dream. I just couldn't get it through to her. And anyway there was no point. She was too pissed to listen or even care. She went back to bed and I got in with Luke.

SCENE 9.

Breda has hung up her blue coat and is dressed up to go out on the town.

BREDA. That day before our night out I went into to town and bought meself a new rig-out, a little black number with fishnet tights, and I went to the hairdressers, just the local and had me hair done. The salon was full of the blue rinse brigade but fuck it, I didn't care. I said to Shane, who did me hair just don't fucking send me out looking like one of them. Don't want to scare the fella's off now, do I? Shane said I should wear some false eyelashes, for a different effect like, so I did. They looked gorgeous. I thought they took years off me. I felt like Elizabeth Taylor, until one of the owl' ones piped up:

WOMAN *(sat on a chair, as if in a salon having her hair shampooed.)* Don't want to look like a slag now do I?

BREDA. The fuckin' cheek of 'er. I was mortified. I wanted to kill her. Reef her hair out of her head. But I couldn't do that, not to an old dear. Not there anyhow. Show meself up like. Fuckin' bitch. You see, I'd just moved back in with me mother. Me and the kids so I couldn't be getting into any trouble. I shouldn't have left the house. My house that is, but I couldn't stay. Jesus we'd made a mess. You couldn't bring two kids up in it. It's a corporation house. So I was waiting on another to come through for just me and the kids. Meantime I was at me Ma's. She didn't mind. She was lonely ye see. The kids gave 'er something to live for since me Da died.

Beat.

Me poor Da. He got knocked down, on his way home from the pub. Fortunately, he was out of his head, so at least

he had a quick end, and he didn't feel anything; but me
mother was devastated. I wasn't sure how I should feel.
Me Da wasn't always there. I just wanted to wipe it out.
Anyway we got out in the end and dropped into Fernando's
for a pre-club drink. It's nice in there, all glitzy like. Gets
you in the mood for a dance.

She dances.

You know what I mean like. Bought ourselves a nice
sophisticated drink, a nice Dubonnet, and got ourselves
psyched up for the club. We were having the craic, until
Noreen gets chatted up, and pulled. She always pulls.
Makes me sick. I mean for fucks sake, I'm the one that
needs fucking chatting up around here, but jaysus when
the fella turned around on his stool and we got a really
good look at him. I nearly died, he was disgusting looking,
he looked about 90 and he could've been Rocky's Da, no
thanks very much, I said to meself. She could have him.
The saliva was running out of the side of his mouth for fuck
sake. And he never stopped talking about what was going
on up North, saying they shouldn't be complaining, that
they had it easy. Everything was much cheaper than down
South. Never mind the troubles like. That didn't matter.
Fucking Gob-shite.

Beat.

Clare, through no fault of her own kept saying.

CLARE. Ah go 'way. Ah go 'way, Jesus that's frightening.

BREDA. And of course, he went on and on, delighted with the interest like. I'll tell you one thing for nothing, we certainly weren't in the mood for a chat about the North. we just ignored him, and then cause we did that, he started slagging us off.

MAN. Go on you pack of whores.

BREDA. We just roared laughing and off we went. We were on our way to a new club called the Blue Lagoon. All the women at Brands, the bra factory, said it was good. They said the men were gorgeous, very exotic looking, and that there were loads of Italians. Pulling an Italian was better than pulling an Irish fella any day. And believe me that made a change from some of the fella's around our way. They were bowzy's, and always in the pub, not an ounce of romance in them. Noreen twisted me arm to go. She said that it would cheer me up- help me forget the imbecile and all the fucking shite that came with him. The shite he put me through. We're in the club having a ball, and it was packed out and I see this fella and he's fucking gorgeous now, and yeah he's Italian. Suddenly I'm on a mission. I'm determined like I've never been before like. When I saw him, I didn't just see a ride for the night, I saw a future. This fella was my ticket out of this kip of a town!. No more bowzy's. No more Rocky. No more shite weather. I was already on a beach somewhere in Italy. Sharing tagliatelle with his mother. Sitting in front of a sea view and speakin' the lingo. I was in me element. I had a white bikini on, and I was black already. He came over and asked me up for a dance. I was scarlet. He was even more gorgeous close up. There we were, on the dance floor, like in Saturday Night Fever or something and giving it all we got. I was very excited. I'd pulled a fella for the first time since Rocky. There was life after!

Gutted

SCENE 10.

Delores is still wearing her bright pink debutantes dress.

DELORES. The double-decker bus came to pick us up. We saw it out the window with everybody queueing up to get on it. Then it was all very exciting. Asumpta's Da got his old camera out, and took a photo of us. *(Laughs)* The fuckin' sap. You could tell he hadn't been to a do for fuckin' ages. I felt sorry for him, and I wanted to bring him along but I couldn't. Jaysus, Anto would have been mortified, and Asumpta would've never forgiven me if I'd of done that. For Christ sake he would've stuck out like a sore thumb. Asumpta's Da is lovely. He's always treated me like his own daughter, and my Da? Well, he had so many kids from so many different women, from so many caravan sites, that he couldn't remember where he lived, let alone how many kids he had. I've lost count meself. Sure the other day, some fella came up to me in the street and said, *(Imitating fella)* 'Howaya, my name's Declan and I'm your Brother'. For Christ sake. What's a girl suppose to do? I was mortified so I just ran. The poor fella. I mean, it's not his fault. Is it? My Da couldn't handle the reality of his life so he drank himself into oblivion. Once when he was really pissed, he asked me who my mother was. Jesus. So there we were, the whole lot of us going to the ball on a double-decker bus if you don't be minding. Excited and mortified all at the same time. And the fella's, well they were scarlet, in their rig-outs. But they couldn't wait to get their girlfriends down the back of the bus, and get their hands up their dresses before ye could even find a seat for yourself. Anto wasn't like that, he was a real gentleman. He wouldn't touch me unless I wanted him to. The thing was I was dying for him to, but I couldn't let on now. Could I? Asumpta and Tomo were already getting off with one another down the back, and they were not letting on. Jaysus the noise of them. While they were at it, Anto

started talkin' to me. I couldn't believe it when he asked
me about where I came from? He said he knew I used to
be a gypo, and that I was from the backfields of Finglas.
I was mortified. I thought nobody knew and now I knew, it
wouldn't be long before everyone else knew about it. So I
begged Anto not to say anything. He promised he wouldn't,
and that he still liked me anyway. So I asked 'im if he was
still going to be his date at the debs and he said.

ANTO. Are ye joking me? Of course I am, ye sap.

DELORES. That was a relief cause, I nearly had enough money
saved from working in the factory. You see, I had this
big plan. That I was gonna save enough money to go
away, and start a new life. Get meself a decent job in
London. So I didn't want anything spoilin' it. And if it came
out that I was a gypo, I'd lose me job and that'd be the end
of my dream. So I knew, if I gave it to Anto, shagged him!
He'd probably keep his mouth shut. So I started feeling him
up, and wearing the face off him, just to get him going!
Before we knew it we were at St Augusta's. The bus
emptied before you could even get your knickers up.
I was desperate to get inside. The hall was huge, but cold.
It was packed with loads of different coloured dresses, and
black suits. Everyone was really excited, and the queue
at the bar was huge. You waited about half an hour, just to
get served and you were that desperate for a drink that you
didn't care. The music was fuckin' brill, and they played
a lot of new romantic stuff; the Human League, Soft Cell,
Tainted Love - my favourite - and ABC. We were in our
element. Asumpta and Tomo liked the slow sets, so
they had an excuse to wear the face of each other. Jaysus,
when Woman came on, you know that John Lennon track,
they nearly ate the face of each other. To be honest I was
a bit jealous, cause Tomo, looked like a good kisser. Anto
was crap. His kissing was all wet and sloppy and he'd stick
his tongue so far down your fucking throat that you'd

nearly choke on it. So I didn't encourage it. I let him neck me a bit, but that was it and I could only do that for so long cause me neck was starting to get love bites all over it. I had enough of that so me and Asumpta went into the toilets. The queue was as long as today and tomorrow. We were nearly wettin' ourselves. Over in the corner there was a bit of a commotion. One of the girls ripped her tights and another girl, was trying to help her sort them out with a bit of nail varnish to stop the ladder getting bigger. When suddenly this other bitch came over, and ripped the whole pair of tights off her. All the way from the top of her legs, to the bottom. The poor girl was in shock, and so was everyone else. Afterwards we heard that the girl whose tights were ripped off, had got off with the other girls fella, when she wasn't looking. It turned out, that it was more than that and that the girl was now pregnant. She's now having to go to London for an abortion. The girlfriend was pissed off and who can blame her. She had to have someone to blame. When we went back out to the dance floor, the slow set was finished. Thank god for that. We all went and sat back at our tables. Then a fight broke out. And it was really bad. There was some fella on crutches, and all we could see from where we were sitting was the fella beating up some other fella with his crutch. God it was terrible. All the girls started screaming. Then the girlfriends of the fella's started fighting as well. One was swinging the other around by the hair, and it was terrifying just to watch. It just got worse and worse, and bigger and bigger and before we knew it everyone was leggin' it out of the hall. You could've easily got killed. There was bottles flying everywhere. Jaysus, you had to duck to miss them. We got outside and we were all loaded onto the bus. The night was cut short, fucked up by a bunch of troublemakers. We were so gutted. Everyone on the bus was quiet and a bit miserable, until someone invited a load of us back to a house party.

SCENE 11.

Deirdre is dressed for work.

DEIRDRE. I'd been trying to forget about that night. Trying to pretend it hadn't happened. I didn't want to upset me Ma, not that she would've believed me. I just kept it to meself. Except one time when I told Delores from work. You could trust Delores. She wasn't like the other girls. I suppose she had secrets of her own. The whole thing was so fucked up because the thing is, I didn't even know who did it. There were so many people in the house that night. So what could I say? But I kept puking in the mornings on the way to school, and in the evenings in this place, and one day Delores made me take a test in the toilets and well, I'm pregnant. When I told me Ma she battered me around the place, told me she couldn't afford to look after me let alone a baby and couldn't afford to send me to England to get rid of it. I took on some extra shifts in the factory and prayed everyday that I'd lose it. I think me Ma did as well and who could blame her? I felt sorry for her until I found out that she was doing drugs with Elvis. Things got more serious between them and before you know it he was moving in. And there I am getting bigger and bigger and everyone's talking about me. There's all sorts of stories going 'round about me at work and one of them is that it was him. Yeah him. Elvis. And the thought of it makes me sick. And believe me, I'm sick enough as it is. I kept going over and over it in me head. It couldn't be him. He wasn't even there that night. It had to be one of Rowena's friends, one of those fellas. It couldn't be him. Then one night I wake up and he's standing at the end of me fucking bed. And I just SCREAM me head off so loud and me Ma runs in the room and she's looking at him and she's looking at me and the penny drops. She starts beating him round the head pushing him down the stairs roaring at him.

MOTHER. Get the fuck out of here you fucking bastard!

DEIRDRE. But it didn't last long. She took him back again after a while cos he could give her what she really wanted. The pair of them wound up in Mountjoy doing time for drugs.

Sharon Byrne

SCENE 12.

Breda is still dressed up for a night out.

BREDA. Me heart stopped when I saw Rocky coming in. I couldn't
believe Rocky turned up. My night out with the girls was
about to be ruined, and any chances I had with the Italian.
The Italian's name was Roberto. Ah Jesus... I was, I was
weak at the knees when he spoke to me. His accent
was very sexy, but all the time I was listening, I could feel
I was being watched. Rocky didn't look that drunk, but I
knew there was going to be trouble. Roberto pulled himself
close to me, and asked me in his gorgeous Italian accent -

ROBERTO. Breda, what is the matter? You look so worried.

BREDA. He could see I was suddenly a bit nervous but I said
nothing. I didn't want him to know too much about me.
I just said that I saw an ex fella of mine, that, that it was
nothing. Roberto said that he's seen me before in the club,
a long time ago and that he fancied me then. I couldn't
believe it cause, it was probably the last time I went out
with Clare and Noreen and that was about a year ago.
I knew he liked me and I was thrilled. Delighted, couldn't
believe me luck. So we went and had a drink over at the
bar. Noreen and Clare were having a right old laugh with
some other girls and fella's they knew. Noreen clocked
Rocky and warned me that I had to tell Roberto what was
going on. So I told him about me and Rocky, and the kids.
I just thought if he knew everything then he'll either stick
around or he'll just piss off. But he stayed. For a while,
Rocky lurked over at the other side of the club. I could sort
of get a glimpse of him now and then, between the crowds.
He was keeping his distance, but I wondered how long
it was going to last. You see he'd been pestering me at
me mothers for weeks trying to get me back. Making all
these promises that I knew, for God's sake, he'd never

fucking keep. Sure I even went over to him one day and tried to talk to him, civil like, but it was no use. Rocky didn't know how to talk. He could only shout and I couldn't stand it any more. I told him to get help, and when I said that he went for me in the middle of the fucking street. I was mortified. Luckily my brother Seano was at home, and he saw what happened and came out and kicked the shite out of him. That was all Rocky knew. It was hilarious, cause when Rocky saw Seano coming out he shit his pants. He kept saying.

ROCKY. Come on Seano, we're mates, come on.

SEANO. No mate of mine hits my sister.

BREDA. Rocky tried to run off, but Seano caught up with him. I was delighted. My brother sticking up for me like that, until he started roaring at me too.

SEANO. Why the fuck did you marry that fucking wanker?

BREDA. I didn't say anything, I couldn't. Rocky is a wanker but when I met him I didn't know any better. I was too fucking stupid. And I suppose I did love him once. I just can't remember what that was like, and how I did. How I loved him. Anyway getting back to the club. Rocky was well oiled now, and I was trying to control Roberto. At least until we got out of there. Then next of all I see Seano and some of his mates, coming into the club looking like they've just stepped out of a gangster film. All decked out in their gear. Their leather jackets and their blue jeans, their hair greased back. I got a bad feeling then. Me and Roberto, went and sat in an alcove somewhere. We were kissing and he couldn't keep his hands off me. I was nervous, and I just wanted to get the fucking hell out of there. But he didn't want to go because he came with a load of his Italian stallion friends, and they were all on the pull

and in one car together. I could smell trouble, there was
Seano and his mates, the Italian stallions, and then there
was Rocky. Now, absolutely pissed out of his head, and
raring to go. I went over to Noreen and Clare to
see what was going on, and if they wanted to go but
Noreen was fucking falling out of her standing nearly,
and Clare was eating the face of this fella, like he was
the last man on earth. I was thinking fucking hell. God it's
the first time I'm nearly sober for years, everyone else
around me is fucking legless, and I just want to go
home to me kids and forget all about this nightmare.
I'm on me way back to Roberto, and I run into Rocky
and he starts calling me a slag. Of course I ignore him, but
then he starts following me. I'm thinking, what will I do?
Because I don't want any trouble so I lead him off the main
floor, into a sidebar to try and talk to him. But it's no use
he's not listening. He begs me to come back to him on
hand and knee. I'm afraid to say no - cause if I do he'll
probably punch me. I say yeah, ok but not until tomorrow.
That I'm out with the girls, and I'll ring him. But he's
not having any of it. Oh no. So he starts dragging me out of
the fucking club.

One of the other women starts dragging her off.

ROCKY. You're not fucking ringing me tomorrow. You're bleedin'
coming with me now.

BREDA. Roberto comes over, and tries to stop him, but he's not
having any of it. He starts calling him the N word. He's
fucking Italian for Christ sake. And that's it, a fight breaks
out and all hell breaks loose.

Beat.

DELORES. We went back to somebody's house in town, near
Dorset Street. The party was carrying on until the early

hours. Everyone was pissed. The makeup was running
down the girl's faces, and the fella's faces were covered in
roaring red lipstick, from ear to ear. All any of us were
interested in, was wearing the face of each other, or riding
the pants of each other, whichever came first. We worked
bloody hard enough didn't we? Me and Anto went into one
of the back rooms, and started trying to have it off. But it
was my first time, and I was nervous. It was very fucking
awkward. With that, I was wearing him. But he just wasn't
any good, and I was starting to wonder what he was like
down there too. You know.

Wiggles her little finger in the air / imitates a small penis.

But I was afraid to touch that. So I just let him feel me up
first. And I'll tell ye what, that was fucking strange. I don't
know what all the excitement was about. Jesus, it was like
he had a brillo pad on the end of his hand. I couldn't do
it. I couldn't go all the way with him. He didn't turn
me on at all. He kept putting his tongue right down me
throat as well, and I tried to show him how to do it, but
sure he was just shite and that was all there was to it. I had
enough. So I got up and went into the kitchen, and got
meself a vodka and orange, and then went into one of the
other rooms. Soft Cell was playing, and you could hardly
see in front of you, with the haze of smoke in the air from
the joints that were being smoked. It was mad. I went
looking for Asumpta and Tomo, as you do. And I found
them in a cupboard, with the ironing board and the
hoover. They were riding the pants off each other.
Everywhere I went there was riding going on. Even
in the toilet. I couldn't even go to the toilet. I had to go
out the back garden. And I have a confession to make. I
went in the dogs bowl. I know. I know that's terrible, isn't
it? But I had a thing about just pissing straight onto the
ground on the grass. And I was wearing a dress with loads
of layers, and I didn't want to get the bottom of it wet. It

had to go back to the hire place. On me way back in, I met Imelda Finnegan, you know, the girl from packaging, who's riding me boss. I said to her. You're riding Mr McEvoy, aren't ye?

IMELDA. No. I am not.

DELORES. Ye are so. Don't fucking lie.

IMELDA. Anyway so what if I am? It's none of your business and anyway he's better than all of these eejits. They don't even know how to get it up.

DELORES. They don't even know how to wear the face off ya.

IMELDA. I know what ye mean. Where's your date then?

DELORES. I said he was probably in the toilet pulling himself off. I wasn't interested. From that moment on, we both laughed our heads off, and got on like a house on fire. She even told me, she was fucking Mr McEvoy, just to get an extra bonus at the end of the year. That she'd never had an orgasm in her life.

Beat.

Imelda Finnegan was far from the type. I never thought of her in that way at all, but as the night went on and the laughs, I discovered something about myself. I discovered, that I liked girls too and that Imelda Finnegan would be the first girl I would ever wear the face off in someone else's porch. She was the greatest of all. That night I knew I'd changed, but I didn't tell Asumpta. I couldn't. When she came out of the cupboard, we decided to call it a night, Asumpta needed to get home. I said goodbye to Imelda and said I'd see her at work. Me and Asumpta walked home all the way from Dorset Street. Our feet were killing us.

When we got home, it was nearly six in the morning, and we just fell into bed. The next morning, Asumpta's Ma cooked us a massive Irish breakfast, looking like she'd never left the kitchen. And she probably hadn't. Not since she'd married Asumpta's Da. At that moment, I knew my destiny. It was crystal clear. I was different. I wasn't going to be wearing apron strings.

That morning, I couldn't stop thinking about Imelda.

They sing together. Acapella style. A slower haunting version of Tainted Love.

SCENE 13.

Deirdre is wearing blue coat, cap and wellington boots.

DEIRDRE. So it was just me and Luke for a while and we were doing alright until the baby came. That's right I gave birth to a baby boy. Luke wanted to call him Tom and well, yeah, I liked that name. He's beautiful and I love him but unfortunately he's got a quiff so, there's no need for tests. Sure, he's like him but thank God he's more like me.

SCENE 14.

Breda is still dressed up for the night. Disco lights are flashing.

BREDA. Roberto is bullin'. I'm out of Rocky's grip, trying to keep the two of them apart. My brother Seano comes over with his mates's, and they're always up for a fight for fuck sake.

Enter Seano ready for a fight.

SEANO. Did that fucking bastard hit you again? I'll fucking kill him. Where is he?

BREDA. I tried to stop it. I just wanted to go home. I'm in fucking bits. I can't believe what's happening. Seano pulls me away, and then him and his mates just lay in. Start kicking the shite out of Rocky and Roberto. Jesus, then all these other fucking Italians start interfering, cause of Roberto, and there's absolutely fucking murder. I can't believe what I'm seeing. There's just loads of fella's kicking the shite out of each other! Noreen and Clare come over, to see what's going on, not to mention the rest of the club. And then the bouncer's move in. Noreen and Clare, and me, attempt to get out but the Gardaí turn up. And they're not letting anyone out. Until they find the trouble makers. And that included us. Yep, we got dragged down the station as well. Noreen started slagging off one of the bouncers and that was it. My first night out in fucking ages ruined. We were all down the station, Roberto, Rocky, Seano and his mates. Noreen, Clare and me. I was mortified. I had to ring me mother and tell her the glorious news. And suffer the embarrassment of being called a fucking eejit over and over again. All I could think was, that at least the kids were all right. Yeah I did have a conscience believe it or not. Strange as it seems, I started going out with Roberto after that. I tell you what, it was so different.

We actually had stuff in common. Sure he had a couple of kids of his own in Italy and was separated like me. My dream of sharing a bit a tagliatelle with his mama *(Laughs)* and the sea view may have been more than just a dream. I was starting to believe it might come true.

Gutted

SCENE 15.

The factory floor. The women are back to work.

DEIRDRE. Well me Da moved back in for the fifty third time and me Ma got out of the Joy. They decided to give it a proper go this time. They were both full of remorse about what happened to me. Me Da beating himself up, that he wasn't there to protect me like.

DAD. Jaysus Christ, I'll castrate that bollox. I'll get him knee-capped.

DEIRDRE. I just let him go on deluding himself and say 'Alright Da, whatever'. He's dead good with Tom though. Always singing him Neil Diamond songs to get him off to sleep, Jaysus if I hear 'I am I Said' one more bloody time, but I have to say it did the trick.

Goes over to Tom sleeping, moment with Tom

Tom is such a good little baby. He barely cries at all, he must have known I had it tough enough as it is. Do ya know I had nightmares that he'd be ugly and a lowlife like him but he looks like me! And I, I have to put those thoughts out of me mind. It's how I bring him up that matters most. Isn't it? Yeah it is. I believe that with all me heart. But round here people talk. Neighbours do nothing but bloody talk and it makes me feel like shit. It makes me paranoid, I'm always looking over me shoulder. Just the other day I was on the bus with Tom and there's two old ones sitting behind me going on and on...

OLD WOMAN 1. Oh all the young girls nowadays are getting pregnant at the drop of a hat. They're all getting flats from the corporation and benefits, and I wouldn't mind, but they're just doing it to get away from their scummy parents.

DEIRDRE. And the other one...

OLD WOMAN 2. But sure it doesn't make any difference whether they get away from them or not. Sure they all turn out the same. Alco's and scum-bags like their parents.

OLD WOMAN 1. Oh A leopard never changes his spots.

DEIRDRE. I'm standing there with Tom and they're making me feel like a scumbag, a slag on benefits. But that doesn't apply to us. We won't be getting any bleeding corporation house of our own. We're stuck living with me scumbag parents the kind they're talking about for the rest of me life. I'll never forget around here, there's too many reminders. I want to make something of meself. I want Tom to be more proud of me than I was of my Ma. And I want him to have a proper Daddy, one that doesn't keep coming and going all the time. I didn't do anything wrong. And I'm not going to spend my life apologising.

Gutted

SCENE 16.

Delores enters, joins Deirdre, begins gutting fish next to her.

DELORES. After the debs night out, everything sort of got back to normal. Me and Asumpta went back to working like dogs, doing loads of overtime and hating every minute of it as usual. When I saw Imelda at work she'd keep her distance, avoided me most of the time, in front of people anyway. We certainly could do without that wanker Jerry Kavanagh, slagging us off along with the rest of the Dublin. Secrets aren't kept for long here and being a lesbian! Well, let's just say, it's not popular. I mean having sex before marriage is a crime, a sin. You get a million our Fathers and thousands of Hail Mary's, if you do that. And if ye go to confession, and if ye have the nerve to confess to that, in the first place, and by the way ye don't. Because ye know you'd be in the fucking church all day praying and that you'd probably end up staying the night. So the pressure! Well it was terrible. But I still couldn't resist to see Imelda again. The other day I sneaked around the back of the factory, and met up with her. Imelda looked gorgeous. I knew I wanted to be with her. I would do anything to be her girlfriend. Imelda Finnegan was on a mission like me. She was saving up to get out of Ireland as well. The bonus that she was getting was gonna give her enough money to get to London. She hated the job, her fucked up family, well what was left of it. The worrying thing about Imelda was that she, didn't come from the luckiest of families. Jesus everyone in her family was either dead or about to die. I'm not joking you. Her da died of lung cancer, only in his forties. Her Ma died of obesity and heart failure, a couple of years ago. Her whole family seemed to go down the same road! Her brother had only one leg, for fuck's sake. He got involved in some protection money racket and got his leg blown off. I could understand why she wanted to get away from Dublin. I just wasn't sure I wanted to go with her. I might die! The thing was we couldn't keep our hands off each other, and all we could do was wear the face of each other. And I did feel guilty. It felt wrong but I couldn't help myself. And I wasn't going to any confession. We met at the back of the job. It was our secret hiding place. And that's where we shared our darkest secrets, and made love. I was in-love with her and every chance I got I wanted to see her. I didn't even care she was riding Malachy. Then one day:

Delores turns to Imelda who appears next to her.

IMELDA. Look Delores I like you. I could even love you but this is never going to work.

Gutted

SCENE 17.

Deirdre enters, whips off her blue coat...she's wearing jeans and a top.

DEIRDRE. This is my last day. No more wellies for me. I'm off to London. And Tom's coming with me. Me Aunty May's letting us stay with her for a while and I've signed up for a secretarial course. I'm going to be a PA. When we get on our feet we're going to rent a small one-bedroom maisonette in Kilburn. I'm gonna get Tom into a decent Catholic school and make some decent friends. Who knows I might even get a decent fella? The other day I heard Elvis drank himself to death in the Joy. I think it was relief I felt. I've decided never to tell Tom about him.

SCENE 18.

Breda is wearing her blue coat, cap and Wellington boots.

BREDA. You know that dream. That dream of mine, of Italy and sharing tagliatelle with the mama , in a nice villa, with the nice sea view. Well, I've met the mother! And eh, I think that might have been a bit premature. Jaysus she's the bitch from hell. The mother's awful. My God she's very possessive. Been over already like, to check me out. Doesn't think much of me. She says, *(in broken English)* I'm a no good. Because I don't, eh, cook in a good kitchen, and I don't, eh, cook the Italian food, the Italian way. She tried to show me how to cook. The other day, and we got into a fight and she nearly beat me up. Roberto had to save me. I think we can safely say that we don't see eye to eye at all, and probably never will. But that's ok. At least, I've got a man who loves me, and doesn't beat me up. The Mother might be a problem though! Ah and I've eh met his two kids, Sophia and Paola, and their lovely and they're getting on alright with mine. So we'll see.

DELORES: Imelda Finnegan left the job.

DEIRDRE: London's gonna be loud and exciting.

BREDA. At least Rocky's stayed away.

DELORES. And left Dublin.

DEIRDRE. The noise of the city will drown out my memories.

BREDA. For now.

DELORES. But for a little while.

Gutted

DEIRDRE. Make me forget for a bit.

BREDA. He still sees the kids at me Ma's.

DELORES. I had the time of my life.

DEIRDRE. Forget what that fucker did to me.

BREDA. I'm still gonna see the girls and we've signed up for Taekwondo.

DELORES. And I'm keeping it a secret.

DEIRDRE. And against all odds, Luke got himself into a decent riding school and became a jockey, the little dwarf!

BREDA. I'll tell you one thing, I won't be putting up with any more shite in my life.

They all take off theirs coats and caps and hang them up behind them.

They sing.

The girls go off with The Supremes, 'Where Did Our Love Go' playing in the background.

Lights down.

End

Sharon Byrne

GET IN TOUCH

sharonbyrne196@gmail.com